HAL•LEONARD
INSTRUMENTAL
PLAY-ALONG

AUDIO
ACCESS
INCLUDED

PLAYBACK+
Speed • Pitch • Balance • Loop

ALTO SAX

Disney MARY POPPINS RETURNS

T0068375

MUSIC BY MARC SHAIMAN
LYRICS BY SCOTT WITTMAN AND MARC SHAIMAN

Motion Picture Artwork TM & Copyright © 2018 Disney

Audio Arrangements by Peter Deneff

To access audio, visit:
www.halleonard.com/mylibrary

Enter Code
1745-7605-3928-5047

ISBN 978-1-5400-4587-4

Visit Hal Leonard Online at
www.halleonard.com

Contact us:
Hal Leonard
7777 West Bluemound Road
Milwaukee, WI 53213
Email: info@halleonard.com

In Europe, contact:
Hal Leonard Europe Limited
42 Wigmore Street
Marylebone, London, W1U 2RN
Email: info@halleonardeurope.com

In Australia, contact:
Hal Leonard Australia Pty. Ltd.
4 Lentara Court
Cheltenham, Victoria, 3192 Australia
Email: info@halleonard.com.au

CAN YOU IMAGINE THAT?

ALTO SAX

Music by MARC SHAIMAN
Lyrics by SCOTT WITTMAN and MARC SHAIMAN

3

A CONVERSATION

ALTO SAX

Music by MARC SHAIMAN
Lyrics by SCOTT WITTMAN and MARC SHAIMAN

A COVER IS NOT THE BOOK

ALTO SAX

Music by MARC SHAIMAN
Lyrics by SCOTT WITTMAN and MARC SHAIMAN

6

(Underneath the)
LOVELY LONDON SKY

ALTO SAX

Music by MARC SHAIMAN
Lyrics by SCOTT WITTMAN and MARC SHAIMAN

NOWHERE TO GO BUT UP

ALTO SAX

Music by MARC SHAIMAN
Lyrics by SCOTT WITTMAN and MARC SHAIMAN

THE PLACE WHERE LOST THINGS GO

ALTO SAX

Music by MARC SHAIMAN
Lyrics by SCOTT WITTMAN and MARC SHAIMAN

THE ROYAL DOULTON MUSIC HALL

ALTO SAX

Music by MARC SHAIMAN
Lyrics by SCOTT WITTMAN and MARC SHAIMAN

TRIP A LITTLE LIGHT FANTASTIC

ALTO SAX

Music by MARC SHAIMAN
Lyrics by SCOTT WITTMAN and MARC SHAIMAN

TURNING TURTLE

ALTO SAX

Music by MARC SHAIMAN
Lyrics by SCOTT WITTMAN and MARC SHAIMAN